Shirley Ann Jackson

Published in the United States of America by Cherry Lake Publishing
Ann Arbor, Michigan
www.cherrylakepublishing.com

Content Adviser: Ryan Emery Hughes, Doctoral Student, School of Education, University of Michigan
Reading Adviser: Marla Conn MS, Ed., Literacy specialist, Read-Ability, Inc.
Book Design: Jennifer Wahi
Illustrator: Jeff Bane

Photo Credits: © Orhan Cam/Shutterstock, 5; © Pakhnyushchy/Shutterstock, 7; © Diego Grandi/Shutterstock, 9; © michaeljung/Shutterstock, 11, 22; © Fox Design/Shutterstock, 13; © Everett Collection/Shutterstock, 15; © PopTech/Flickr, 17; © National Science Foundation, 19, 23; © PopTech/Flickr, 21; Cover, 6, 10, 18, Jeff Bane; Various frames throughout, © Shutterstock Images

Library of Congress Cataloging-in-Publication Data

Names: Loh-Hagan, Virginia, author. | Bane, Jeff, 1957- illustrator.
Title: Shirley Ann Jackson / by Virginia Loh-Hagan ; illustrator: Jeff Bane.
Other titles: My itty-bitty bio.
Description: Ann Arbor, Michigan : Cherry Lake Publishing, [2018] | Series:
   My itty-bitty bio | Includes index. | Audience: K to grade 3.
Identifiers: LCCN 2017030504| ISBN 9781534107137 (hardcover) | ISBN 9781534108127
   (pbk.) | ISBN 9781534109117 (pdf) | ISBN 9781534120105 (hosted ebook)
Subjects: LCSH: Jackson, Shirley Ann, 1946---Juvenile literature. |
   Physicists--United States--Biography--Juvenile literature. | Women
   physicists--United States--Biography--Juvenile literature.
Classification: LCC QC16.J33 L64 2018 | DDC 530.092 [B] --dc23
LC record available at https://lccn.loc.gov/2017030504

Printed in the United States of America
Corporate Graphics

About the author: Dr. Virginia Loh-Hagan is an author, university professor, former classroom teacher, and curriculum designer. Like Shirley, she works in a university and wants to support women in STEM jobs. She lives in San Diego with her very tall husband and very naughty dogs. To learn more about her, visit: www.virginialoh.com

About the illustrator: Jeff Bane and his two business partners own a studio along the American River in Folsom, California, home of the 1849 Gold Rush. When Jeff's not sketching or illustrating for clients, he's either swimming or kayaking in the river to relax.

I was born in Washington, D.C. It was 1946.

Where were you born?

I loved bees. I put them in jars.
I watched them.

I was a young **scientist**.

What kind of science do you like?

I went to **MIT**. Few blacks were there.

People were unfair to me. I was lonely.

I didn't quit. I got a **doctorate** in **physics**.

I was the first black woman to do this.

I worked in labs. I studied **particles**.

I did tests. I wrote. I taught.

What can you teach others?

I worked for U.S. presidents.
I gave them ideas.

My choices protected our planet.

I became a **university** president. I was the first black woman to do this.

I won the National Medal of Science. It is for people who do important work in **science**.

I got other awards.

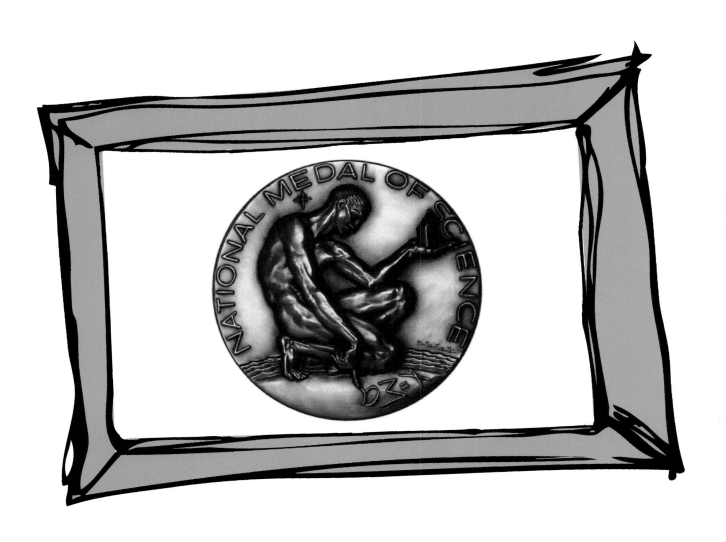

My work helped women.
It helped blacks.

All people can be leaders
in science.

What would you like to ask me?

1973

1940

Born
1946

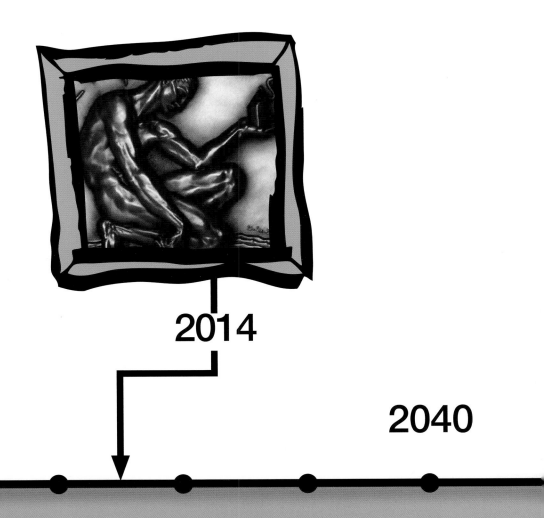

2014

2040

glossary

doctorate (DAHK-tur-et) the highest degree (or title) that can be earned at a university

MIT (EM-eye-tee) Massachusetts Institute of Technology, a college known for teaching science

particles (PAHR-ti-kuhlz) small pieces or amounts of something

physics (FIZ-iks) the study of movement, force, light, heat, sound, and electricity

science (SYE-uhns) the study of nature and the world we live in

scientist (SYE-uhn-tist) a person who studies science

university (yoo-nuh-VUR-sih-tee) a school for higher learning

index